Piano · Vocal · Guitar

THE VERY BEST OF
BILLIE HOLIDAY

LADY DAY: THE SINGER & THE SONGWRITER

Cover photo courtesy of

ISBN 978-1-4950-2804-5

HAL·LEONARD®
CORPORATION

7777 W. BLUEMOUND RD. P.O. BOX 13819 MILWAUKEE, WI 53213

Visit Hal Leonard Online at
www.halleonard.com

BILLIE'S BLUES
(I Love My Man)

Words and Music by
BILLIE HOLIDAY

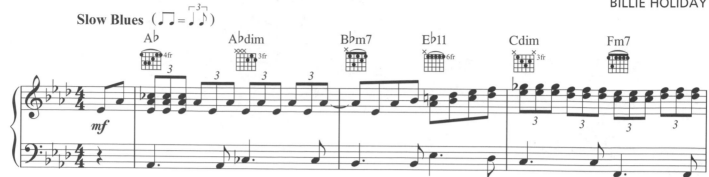

I love my man, I'm a li-ar____ if I say I

don't.____ I love my man,

I'm a li-ar if I say I don't.____ But I'll

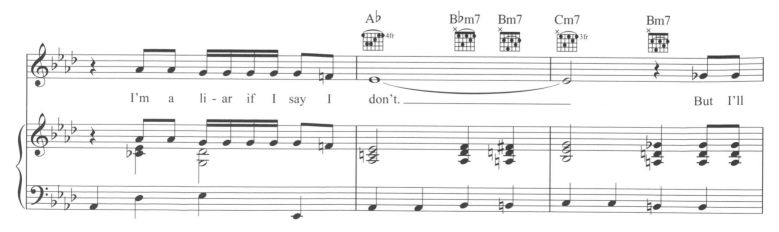

BODY AND SOUL

Words by EDWARD HEYMAN,
ROBERT SOUR and FRANK EYTON
Music by JOHN GREEN

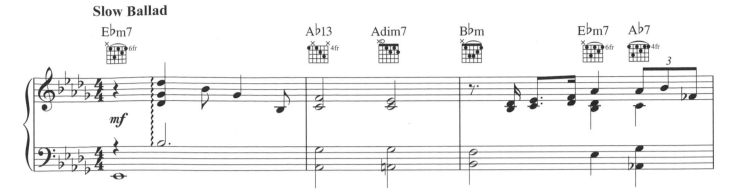

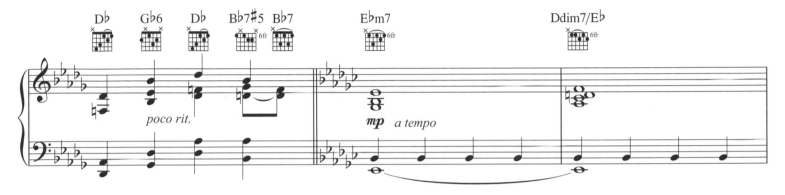

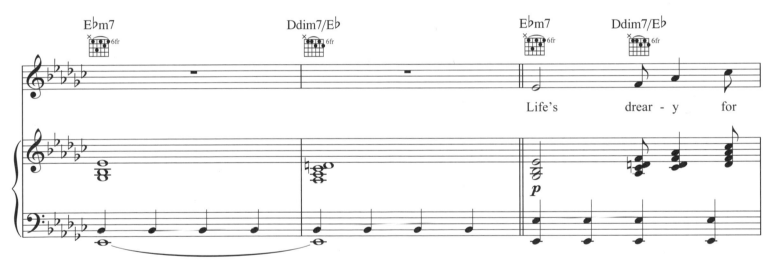

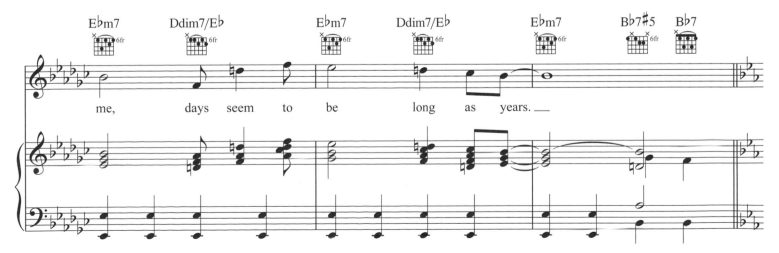

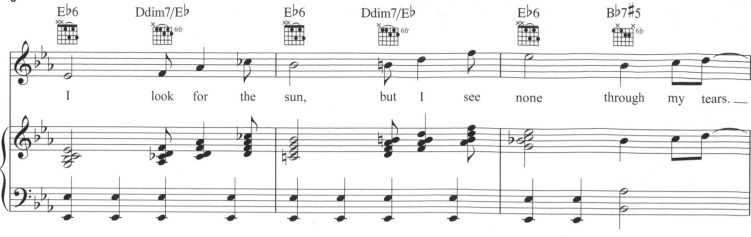

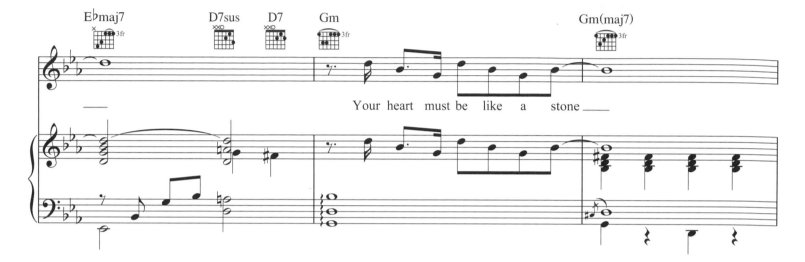

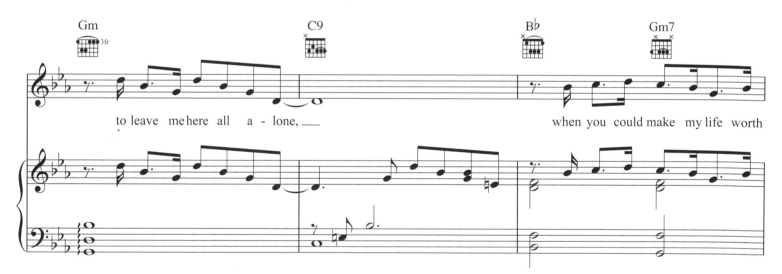

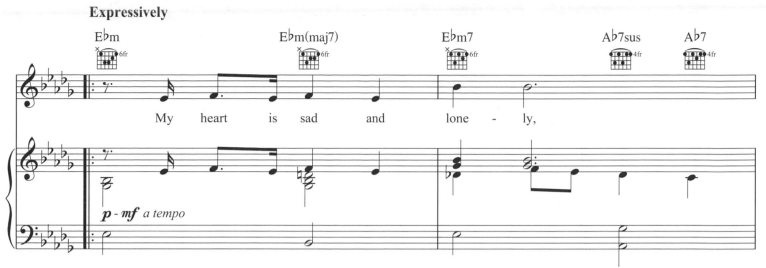

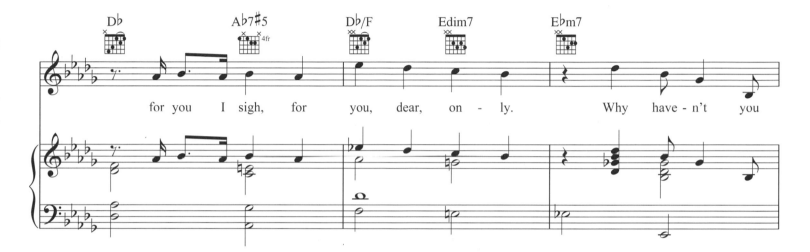

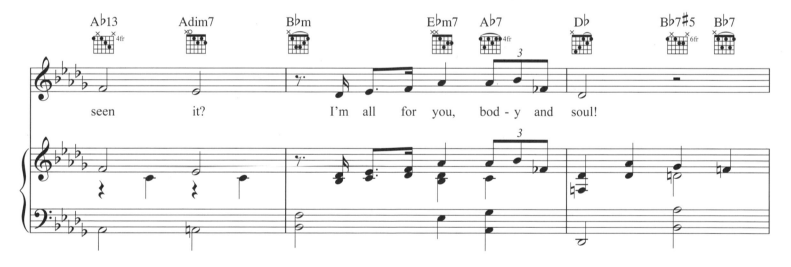

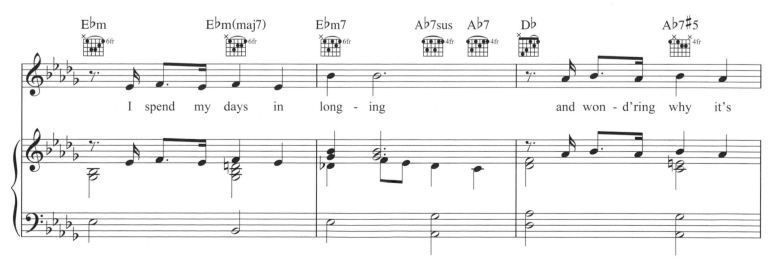

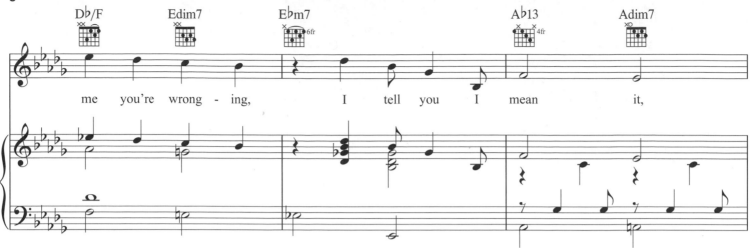

me you're wrong - ing, I tell you I mean it,

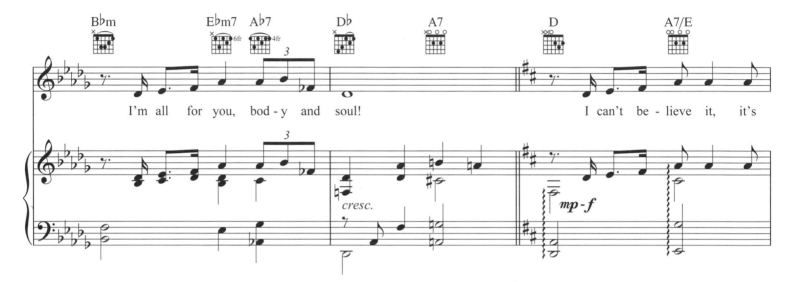

I'm all for you, bod - y and soul! I can't be - lieve it, it's

hard to con - ceive it, that you'd turn a - way ro - mance.

Are you pre - tend - ing, it looks like the end - ing un - less I could have one more

dance to prove, dear. My life a wreck you're mak - ing,

you know I'm yours for just the tak - ing;

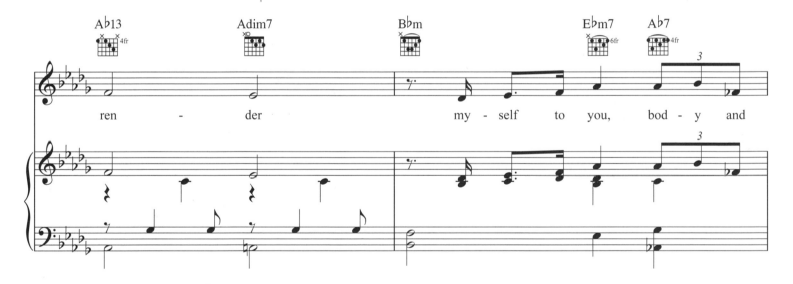

I'd glad - ly sur - ren - der my - self to you, bod - y and

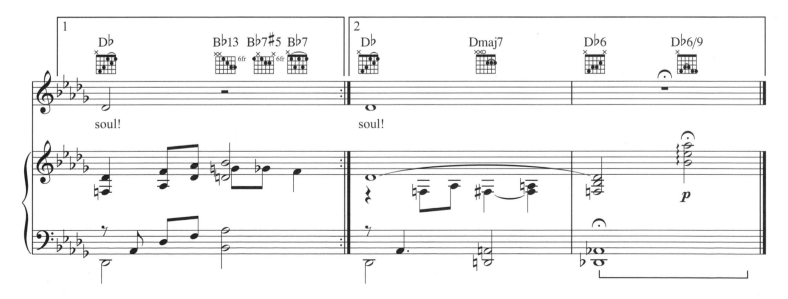

soul!

soul!

CRAZY HE CALLS ME

Music by CARL SIGMAN
Lyrics by BOB RUSSELL

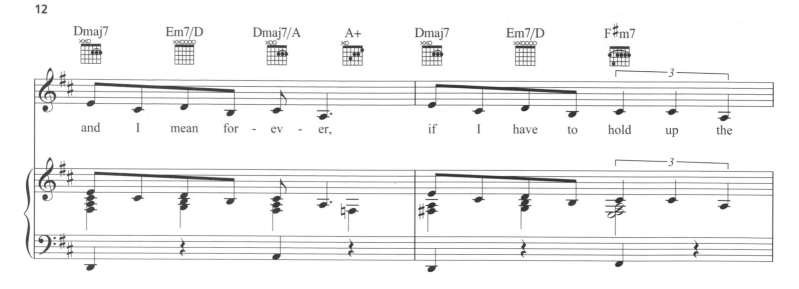

and I mean for - ev - er, if I have to hold up the

sky. "Cra - zy" he calls me; sure, I'm cra - zy,

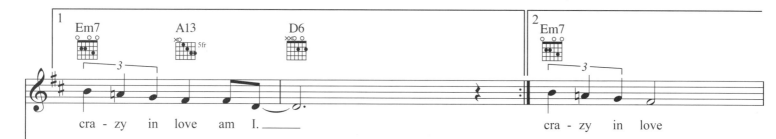

1. cra - zy in love am I. _____ 2. cra - zy in love

am I.

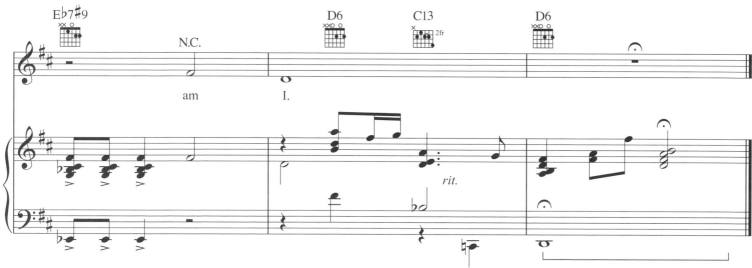

DON'T EXPLAIN

Words and Music by BILLIE HOLIDAY
and ARTHUR HERZOG

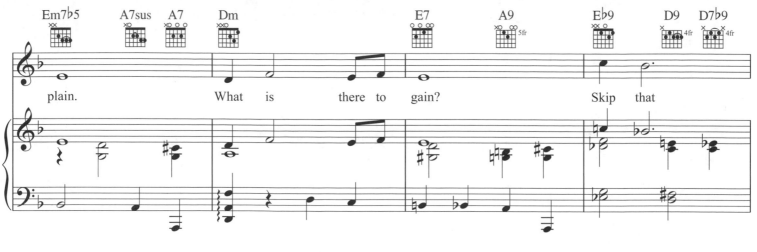

plain. What is there to gain? Skip that

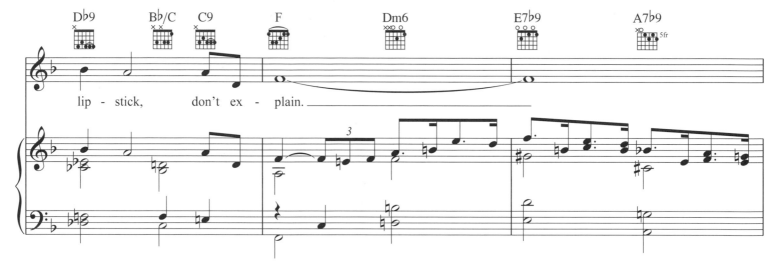

lip - stick, don't ex - plain. _____

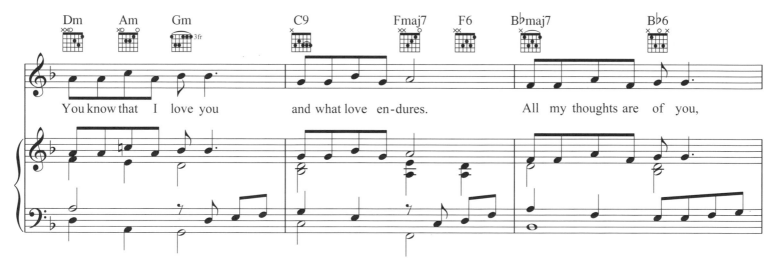

You know that I love you and what love en-dures. All my thoughts are of you,

for I'm so com - plete - ly yours. Cry to hear folks chat - ter, and I know you cheat.

Right or wrong don't mat-ter when you're with me, sweet. Hush now, don't ex -

plain. You're my joy and pain.

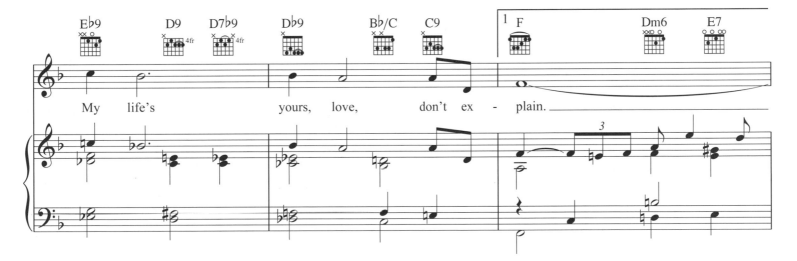

My life's yours, love, don't ex - plain. _____

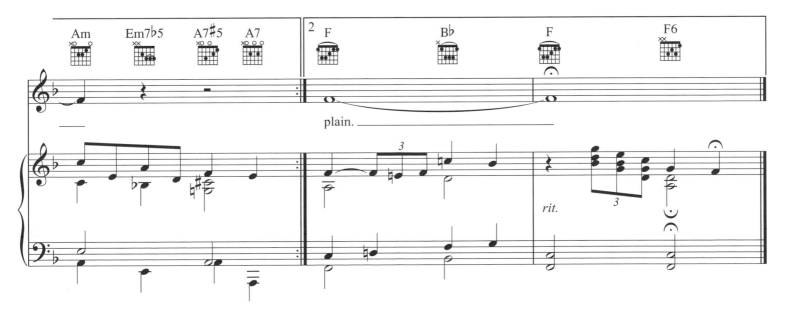

plain. _____

EASY LIVING
Theme from the Paramount Picture EASY LIVING

Words and Music by LEO ROBIN
and RALPH RAINGER

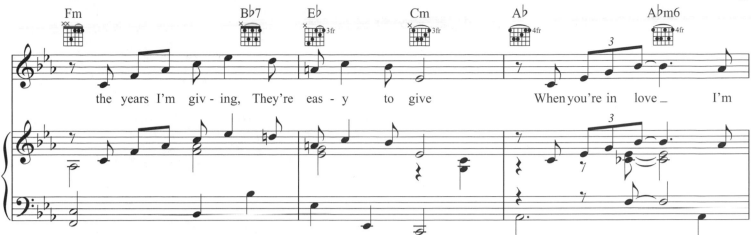

the years I'm giv-ing, They're eas-y to give When you're in love __ I'm

hap-py to do what-ev-er I do __ for you, ____

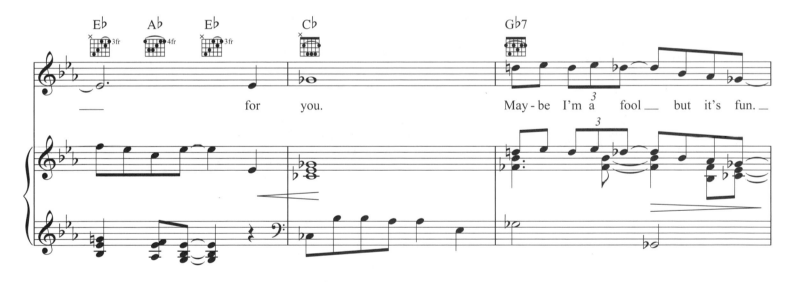

__ for you. May-be I'm a fool __ but it's fun. __

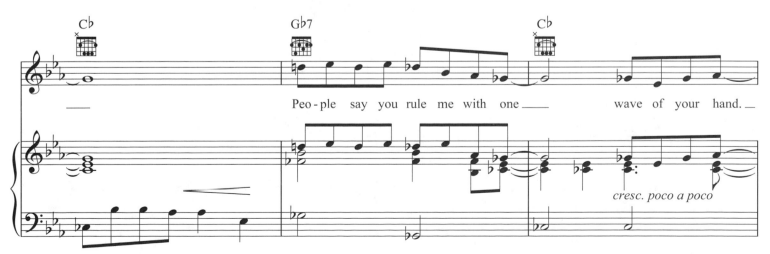

Peo-ple say you rule me with one ____ wave of your hand. __

cresc. poco a poco

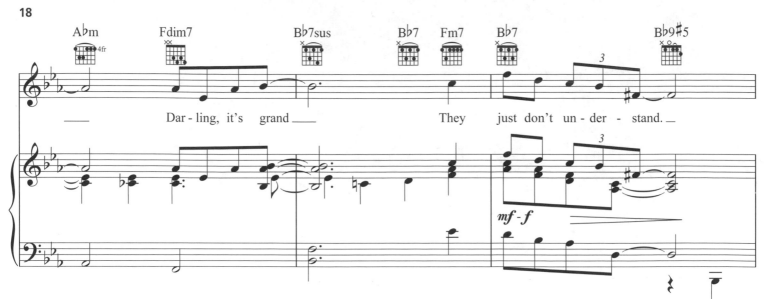

Dar - ling, it's grand ___ They just don't un - der - stand. ___

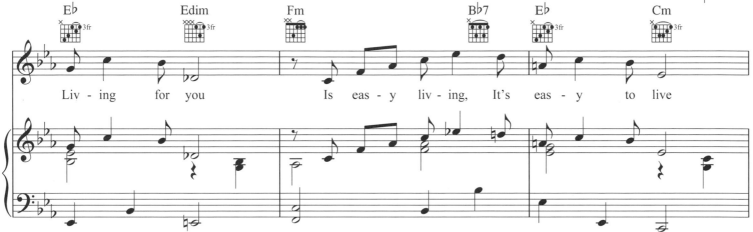

Liv - ing for you Is eas - y liv - ing, It's eas - y to live

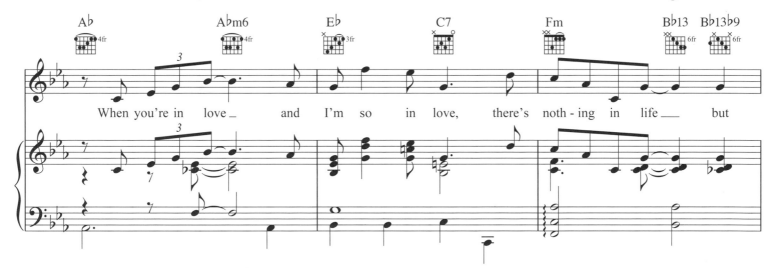

When you're in love ___ and I'm so in love, there's noth - ing in life ___ but

you. ___ you. ___

FINE AND MELLOW

Words and Music by
BILLIE HOLIDAY

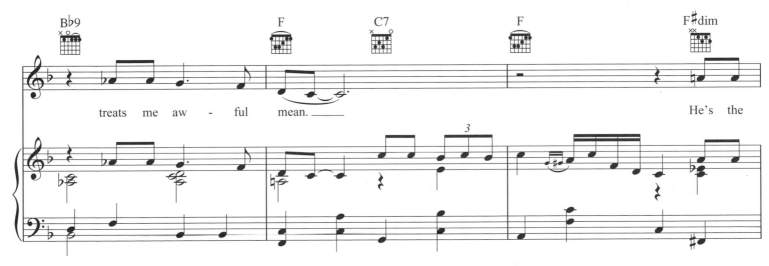

starts in to love me, he's so fine and mel - low. _____

Love will make you drink and gam - ble, make you stay out all night

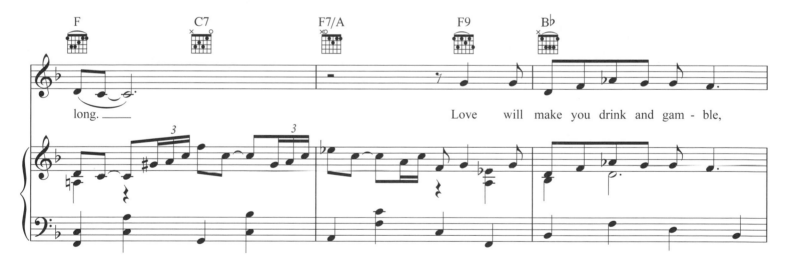

long. _____ Love will make you drink and gam - ble,

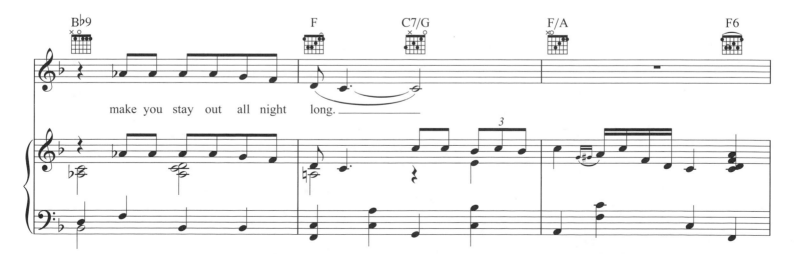

make you stay out all night long. _____

mean to me, ba - by,   I know you're gon - na drive me a - way.   Love is

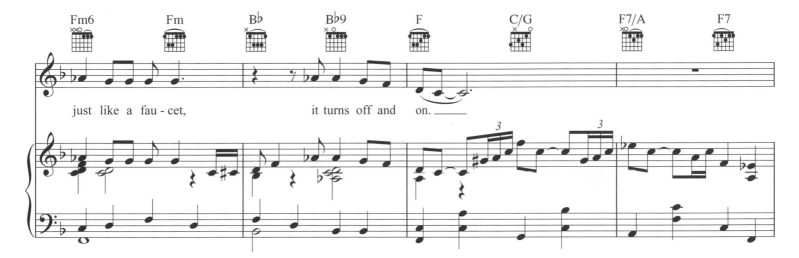

just like a fau - cet,   it turns off and on. _____

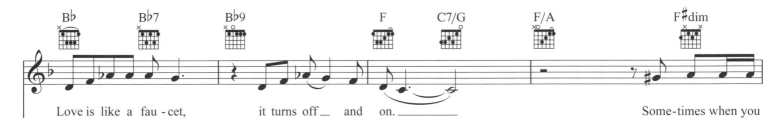

Love is like a fau - cet,   it turns off __ and on. _____   Some-times when you

think it's on, ba - by,   it has turned off and gone. _____

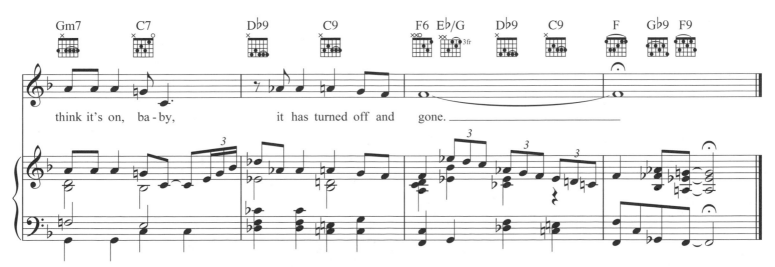

GOD BLESS THE CHILD

Words and Music by ARTHUR HERZOG JR.
and BILLIE HOLIDAY

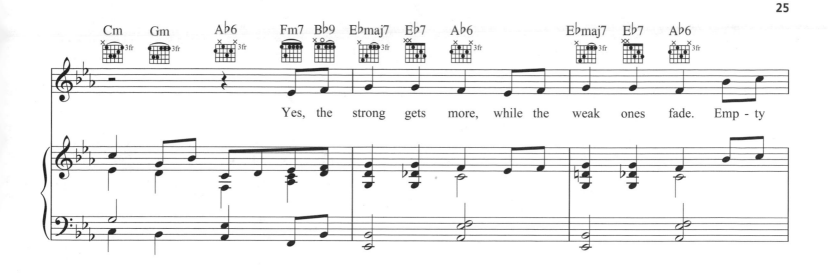

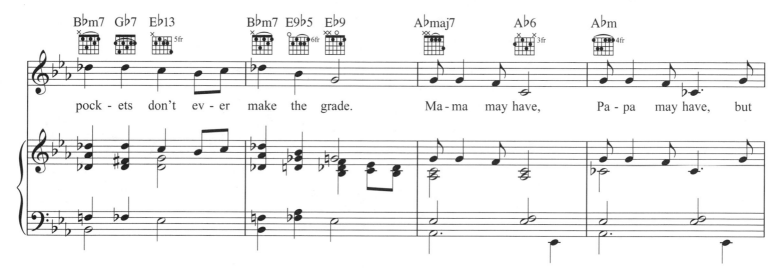

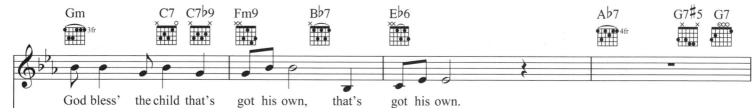

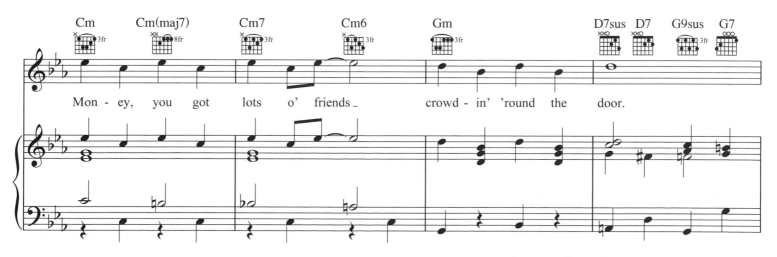

GOOD MORNING HEARTACHE

Words and Music by DAN FISHER,
IRENE HIGGINBOTHAM and ERVIN DRAKE

but you're here to stay. It seems I met you when my love went a-way.

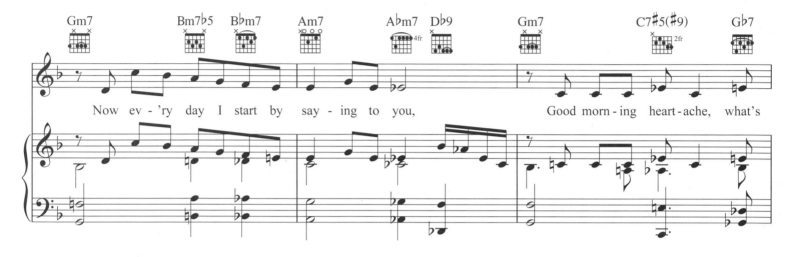

Now ev-'ry day I start by say-ing to you, Good morn-ing heart-ache, what's

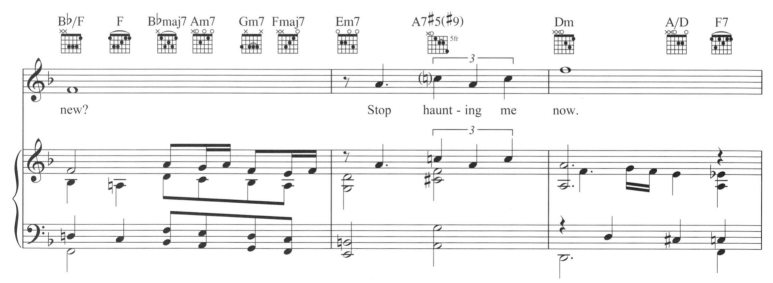

new? Stop haunt-ing me now.

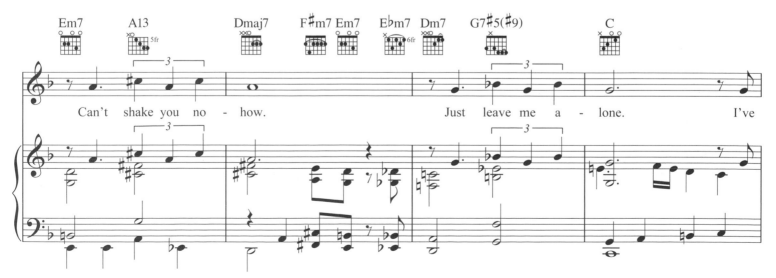

Can't shake you no - how. Just leave me a - lone. I've

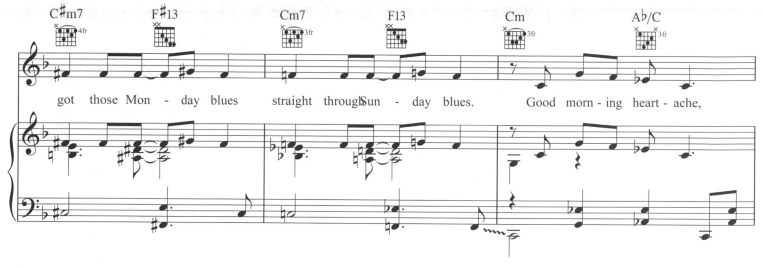

got those Mon - day blues straight through Sun - day blues. Good morn - ing heart - ache,

here we go a - gain. __ Good morn - ing heart - ache, you're the one who knew me when.

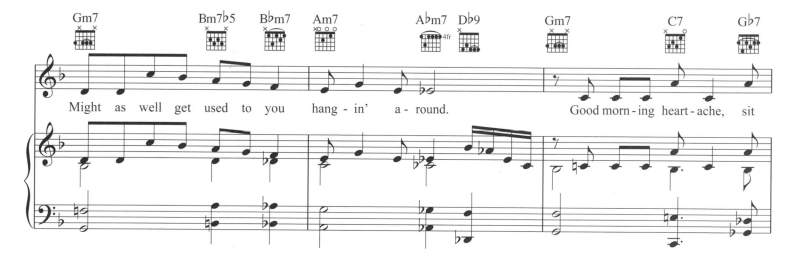

Might as well get used to you hang - in' a - round. Good morn - ing heart - ache, sit

down! down! __

I'LL BE SEEING YOU

from RIGHT THIS WAY

Written by IRVING KAHAL
and SAMMY FAIN

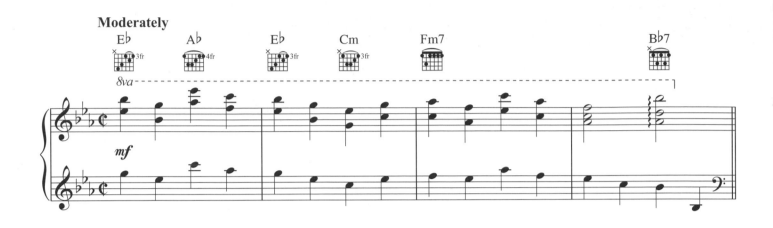

Ca- the-dral bells were toll- ing _____ and our hearts sang

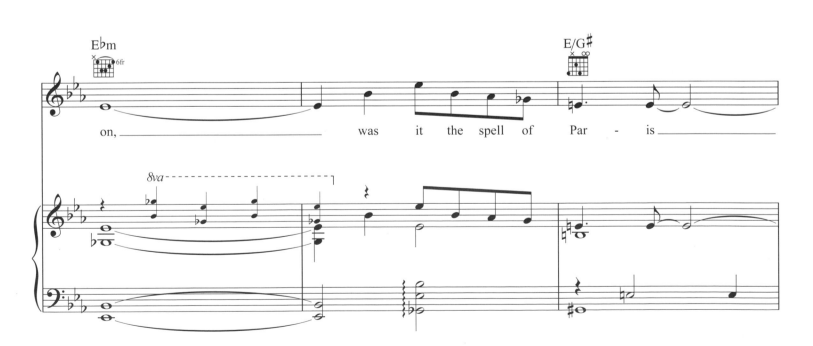

on, _____ was it the spell of Par- is _____

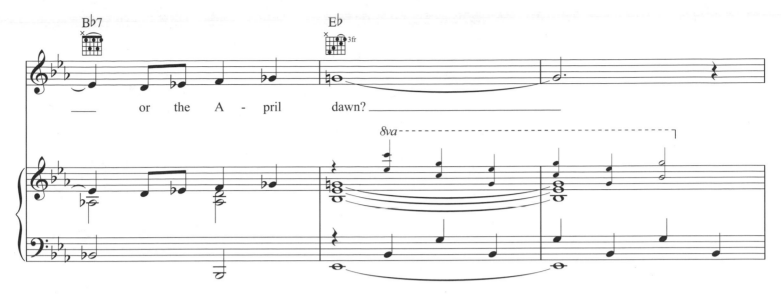

or the A - pril dawn? _____

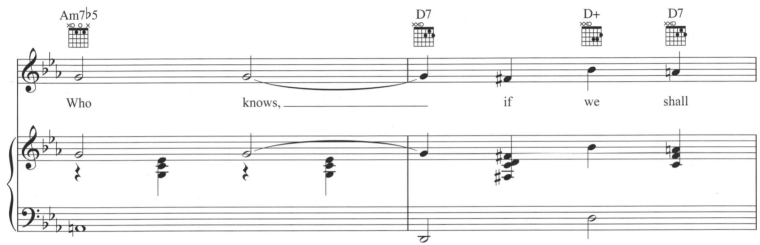

Who knows, _____ if we shall

meet a - gain? _____ But when the

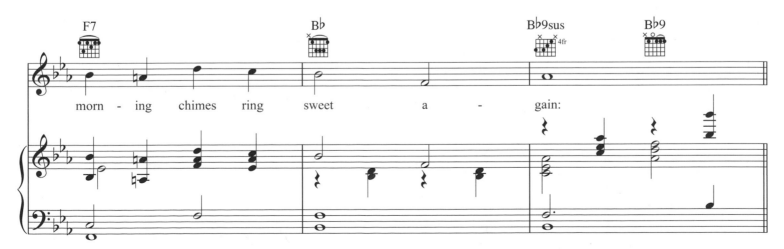

morn - ing chimes ring sweet a - gain:

Slowly

I'll be see-ing you __ in all the old fa-

mil - iar plac - es that this heart of mine em - brac - es

all day through: __ in that

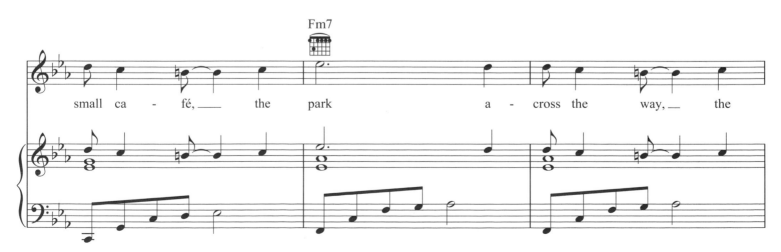

small ca - fé, __ the park a - cross the way, __ the

chil - dren's car-ou - sel, ___ the chest-nut trees, ___ the

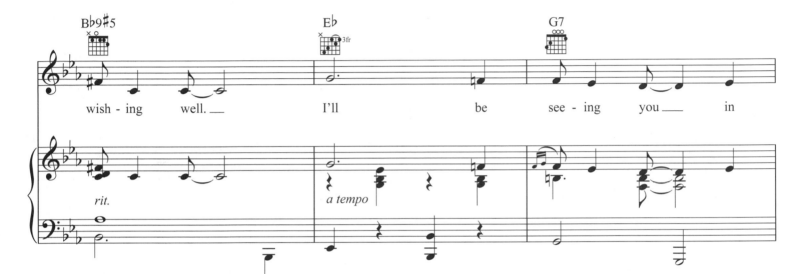

wish - ing well. ___ I'll be see-ing you ___ in

rit.   *a tempo*

ev - 'ry love - ly sum - mer's day, in ev - 'ry-thing that's

light and gay, I'll al - ways think of you that way. I'll

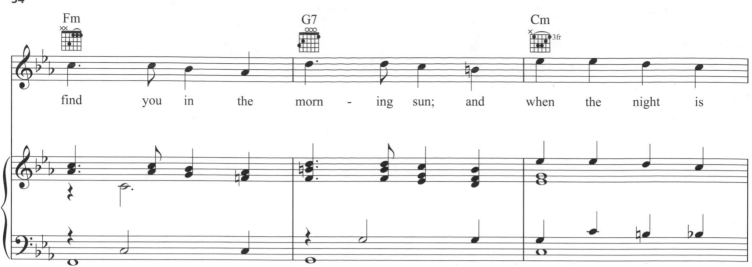

find you in the morn - ing sun; and when the night is

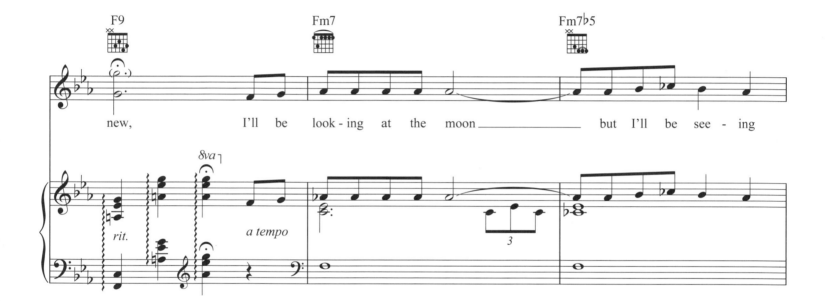

new, I'll be look - ing at the moon _____ but I'll be see - ing

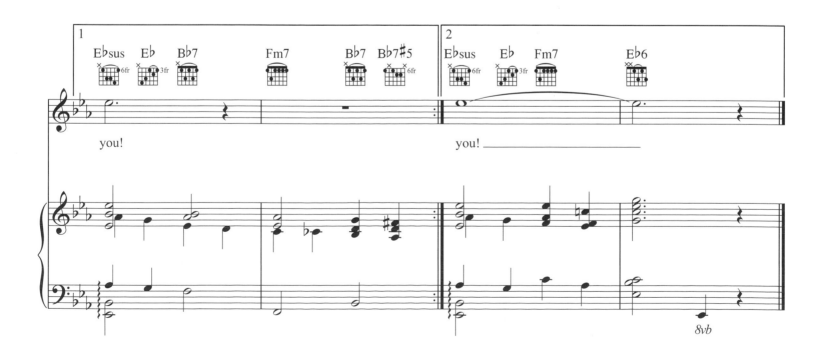

you! you! _____

LADY SINGS THE BLUES

Words and Music by HERBERT NICHOLS
and BILLIE HOLIDAY

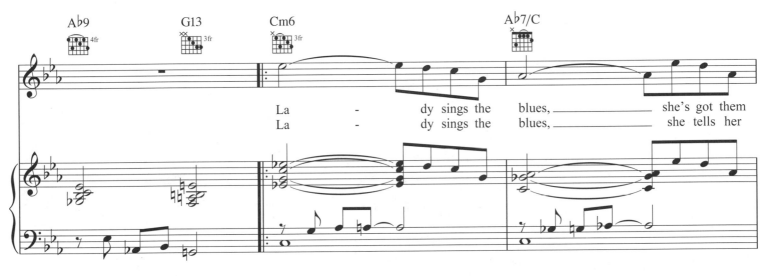

La - dy sings the blues, _____ she's got them
La - dy sings the blues, _____ she tells her

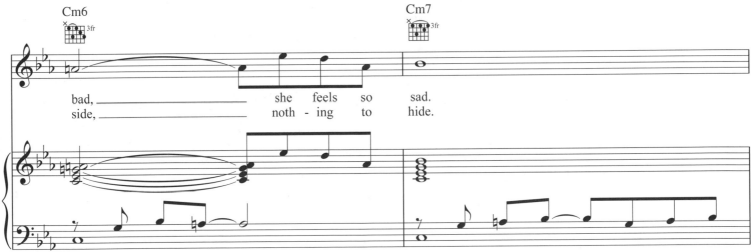

bad, _____ she feels so sad.
side, _____ noth - ing to hide.

Wants _____ the world to know _____ what the blues
Now _____ the world will know _____ just what the

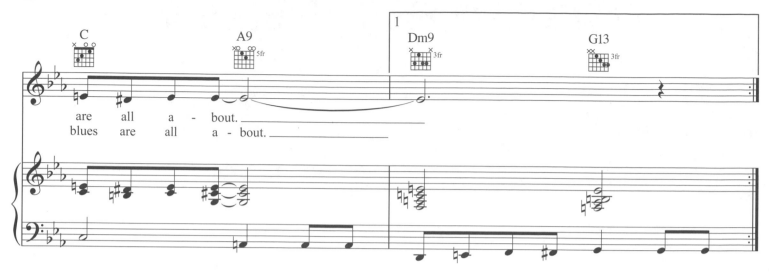

die _____ be - cause she loves him. _____

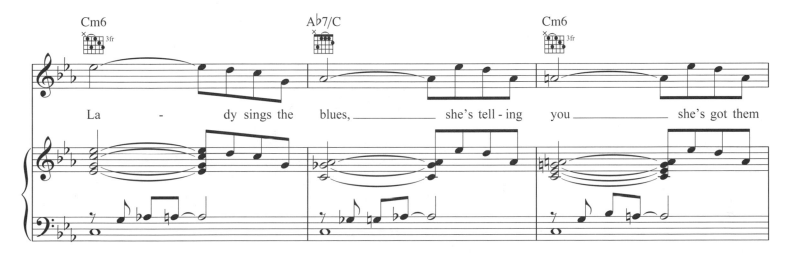

La - dy sings the blues, _____ she's tell - ing you _____ she's got them

bad. Now _____ the world will know, she's

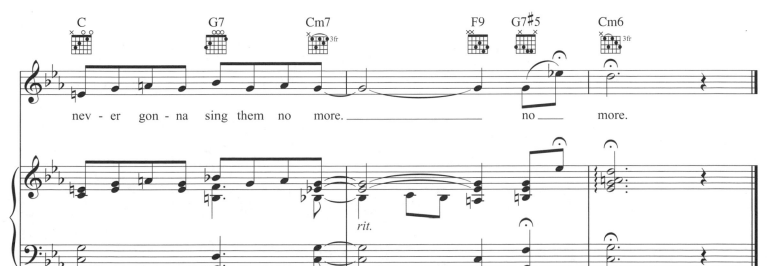

nev - er gon - na sing them no more. _____ no ___ more.

I'VE GOT MY LOVE TO KEEP ME WARM

from the 20th Century Fox Motion Picture ON THE AVENUE

Words and Music by
IRVING BERLIN

Bright jump tempo

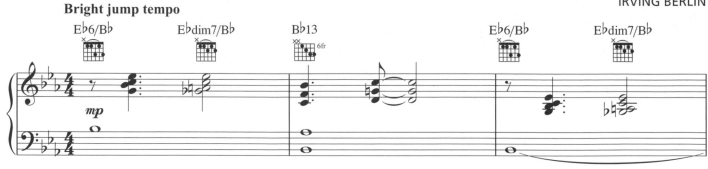

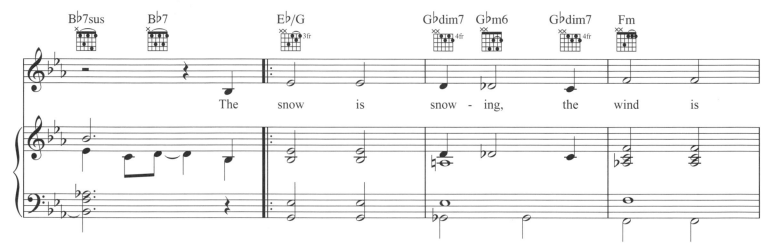

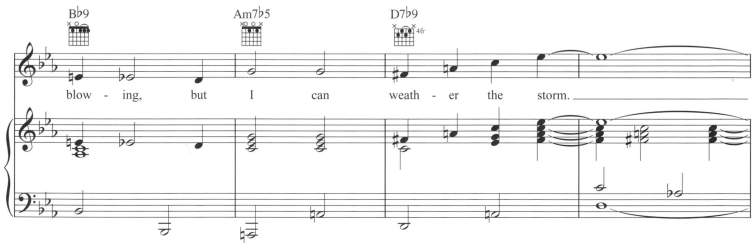

The snow is snow-ing, the wind is blow-ing, but I can weath-er the storm.

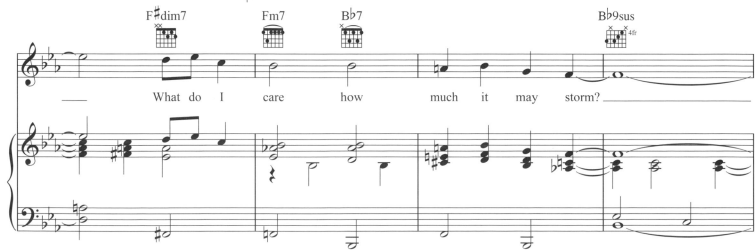

What do I care how much it may storm?

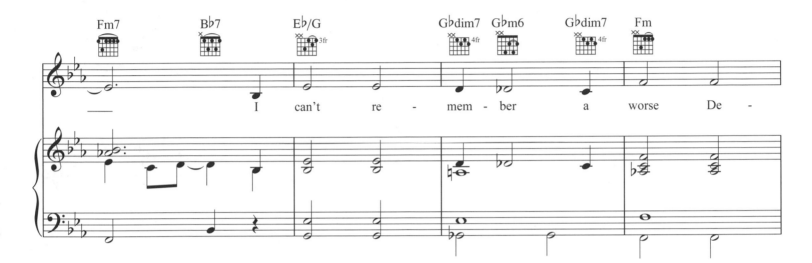

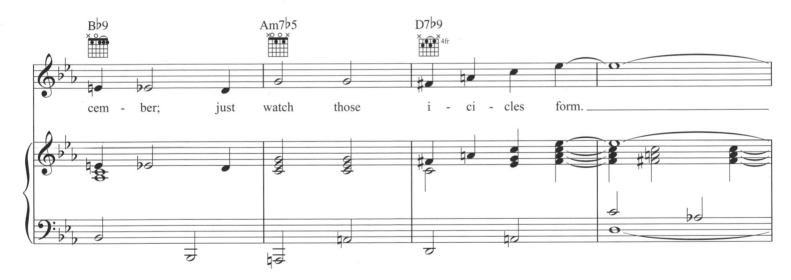

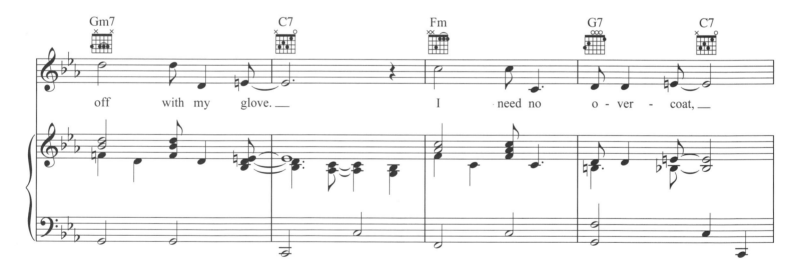

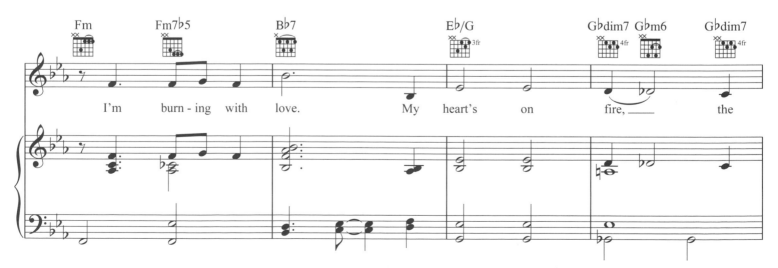

flame grows high - er, so I will weath - er the storm. _

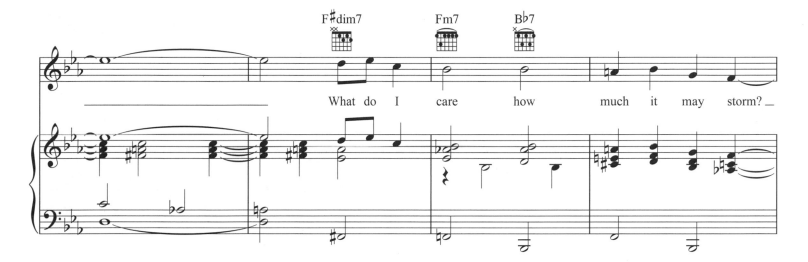

What do I care how much it may storm? _

I've got my love to keep me warm. _

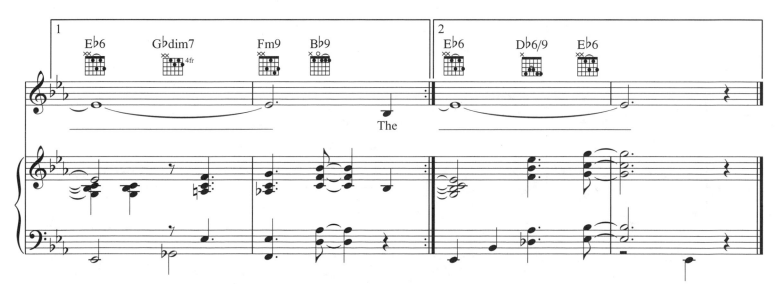

The

IT HAD TO BE YOU

Words by GUS KAHN
Music by ISHAM JONES

Moderate Swing

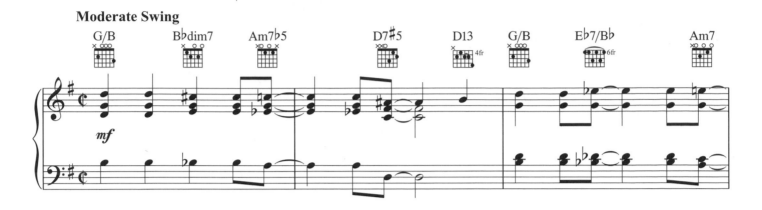

Why do I do just as you say, ___
Seems like dreams like I al-ways had, ___

why must I just give you your way? _
could be, should be mak-ing me glad. _

Why do I sigh, _
Why am I blue? _

why don't I try ___ to for - get?
It's up to you ___ to ex - plain.

It must have
I'm think - ing

been that some - thing lov - ers call fate ___
may - be, ba - by, I'll go a - way, ___

kept on say - ing
some - day, some way,

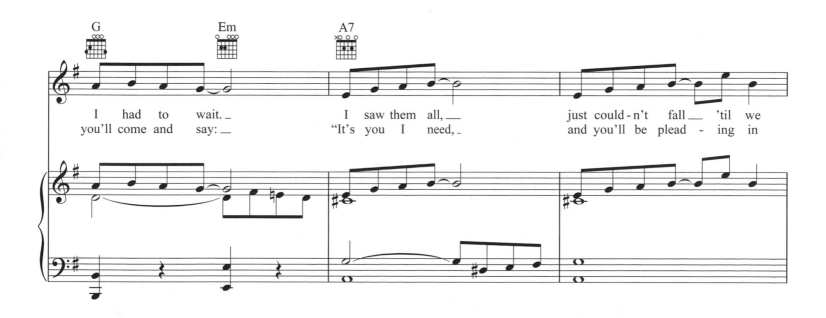

I had to wait. ___
you'll come and say: ___

I saw them all, ___
"It's you I need, ___

just could - n't fall ___ 'til we
and you'll be plead - ing in

met. _____

vain. _____ } It had to be you, _____

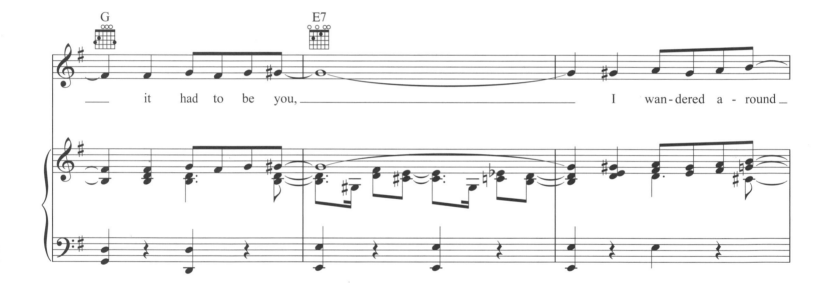

___ it had to be you, _____ I wan-dered a-round ___

___ and fi-nal-ly found ___ the some-bod-y who _____

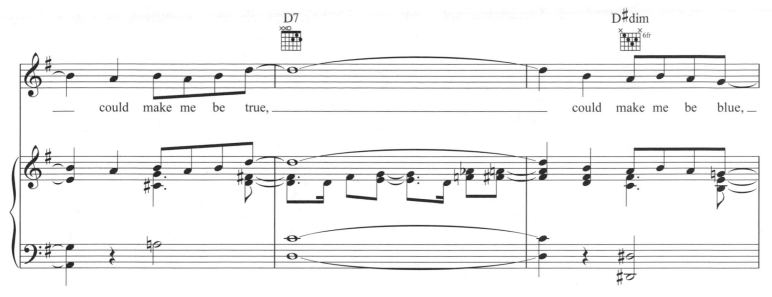

could make me be true, _____ could make me be blue, _

_____ and e-ven be glad, _ just to be sad, _

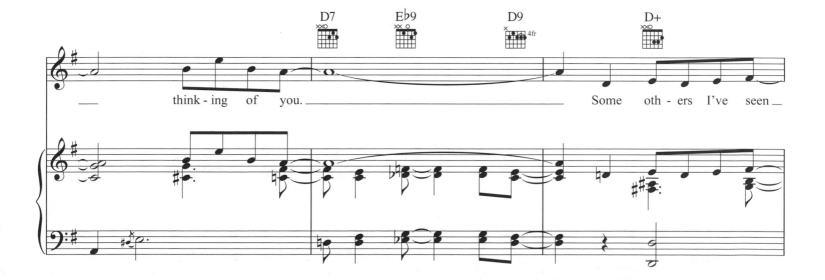

_ think-ing of you. _____ Some oth-ers I've seen _

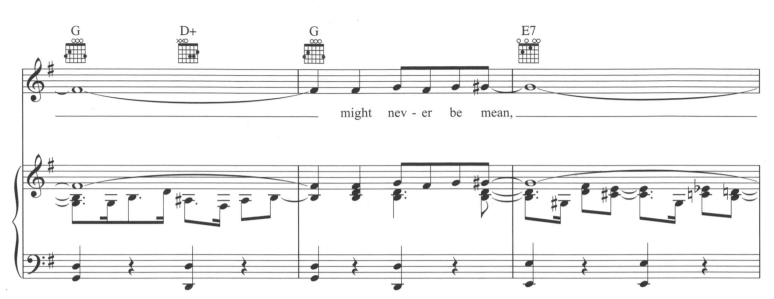

might nev - er be mean, _____

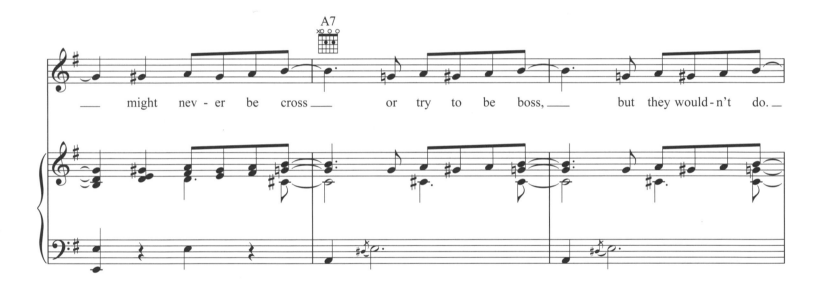

__ might nev - er be cross ___ or try to be boss, ___ but they would - n't do. __

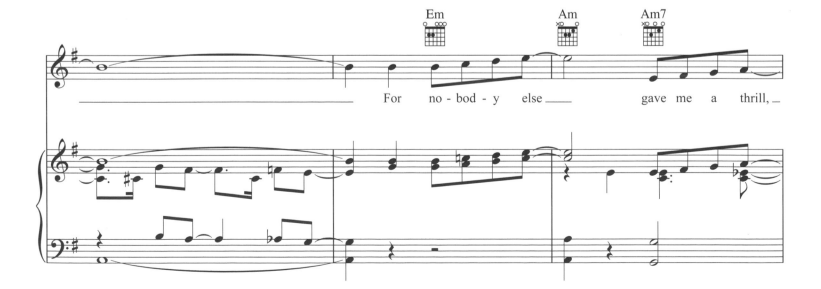

For no - bod - y else ___ gave me a thrill, __

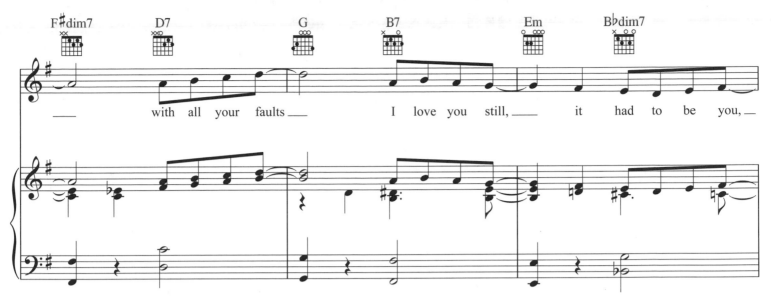

with all your faults ___ I love you still, ___ it had to be you, ___

1

won - der - ful you, ___ had to be you. ___

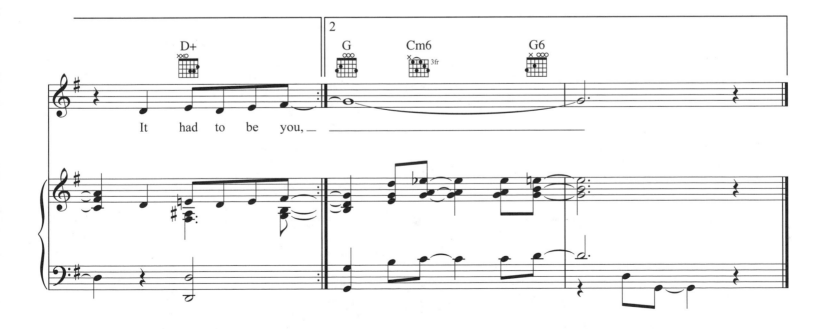

2

It had to be you, ___

LONG GONE BLUES

Words and Music by
BILLIE HOLIDAY

Oh, tell me, ba-by, tell me what's the mat-ter now. ___

Tell me, ba-by, what's the mat-ter now? ___ Are you

try-in' to quit me, ba-by, but you don't know how. ___ I've

been   your   slave _____   ev - er   since I've been your   babe. _____
I'm   a   good   gal, _____   but   my   love   is   all ____   wrong. _____

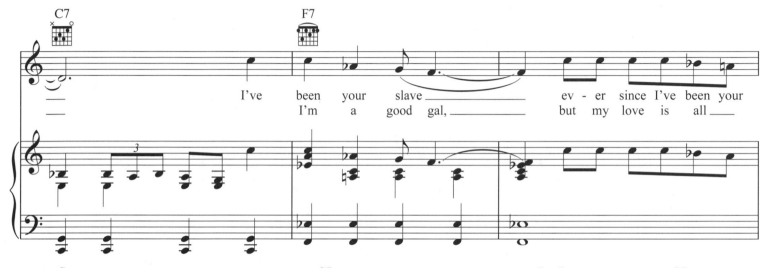

____   I've   been   your   slave _____   ev - er   since I've been your
____   I'm   a   good   gal, _____   but   my   love   is   all ____

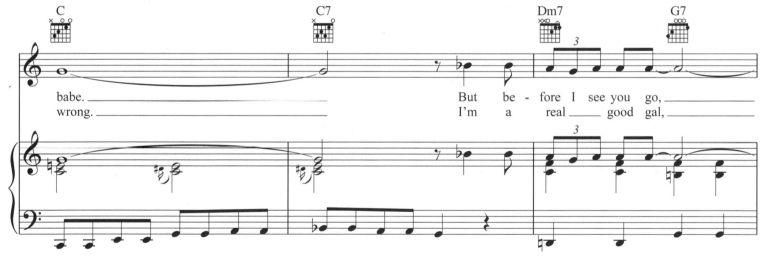

babe. _____   But   be - fore I see you   go, _____
wrong. _____   I'm   a   real ____ good gal, _____

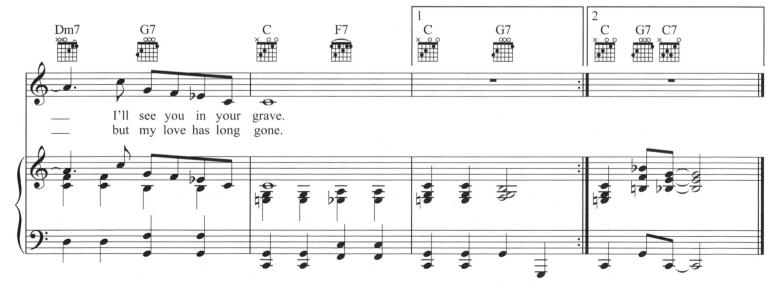

____   I'll   see   you   in   your   grave.
____   but   my   love   has   long   gone.

LOVER MAN
(Oh, Where Can You Be?)

Words and Music by JIMMY DAVIS,
ROGER RAMIREZ and JIMMY SHERMAN

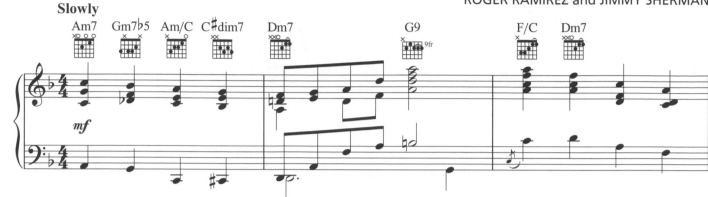

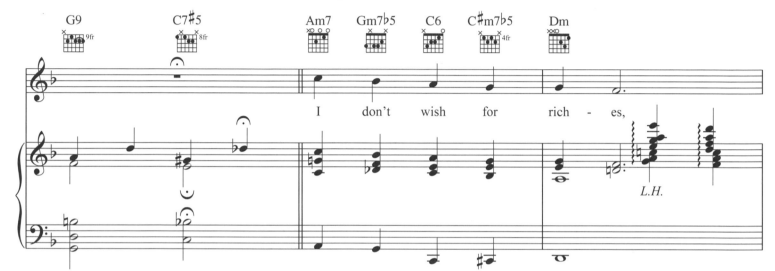

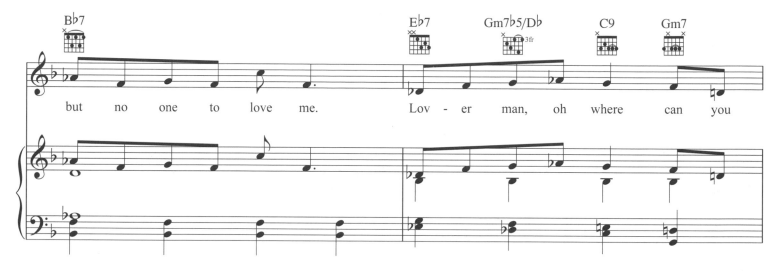

MY MAN
(Mon homme)

Words by ALBERT WILLEMETZ and JACQUES CHARLES
English Words by CHANNING POLLOCK
Music by MAURICE YVAIN

It's cost me a lot, but there's one thing that I've got it's my man, —
Some-times I say if I just could get a-way with my man, —
Sur cet-te terr', ma seul' joie, mon seul bon-heur c'est mon hom-me

cold and wet, tired, you bet, but all that I soon for-get with my man. —
he'd go straight sure as fate, for it nev-er is too late for my man. —
J'ai don-né tout c'que j'ai, mon a-mour et tout mon cœur, a mon hom-me,

He's not much for looks, and no he-ro out of books is my man. —
I just like to dream of a cot-tage by a stream with my man, —
Et mê-me la nuit quand je rê-ve c'est de lui, de mon hom-me.

Two or three girls has he that he likes as well as me, but I love him! I
where a few flow-ers grew and per-haps a kid or two, like my man.__ And
Ce n'est pas qu'il est beau qu'il est ri-che ni cos-taud mais je l'ai-me, c'est i-

don't know why I should, he is-n't good, he is-n't true, he beats me,
then my eyes get wet, I 'most for-get, 'til he gets hot, and tells me
diot j'm' fout des coups, *j'm'prend mes sous,* *Je suis à bout mais mal - gré*

too. What can I do? Oh, my man I love him so, he'll nev - er
not to talk such rot. }
tout que vou - lez-vous. *Je l'ai tell' ment dans la peau qu'j'en d'viens mar -*

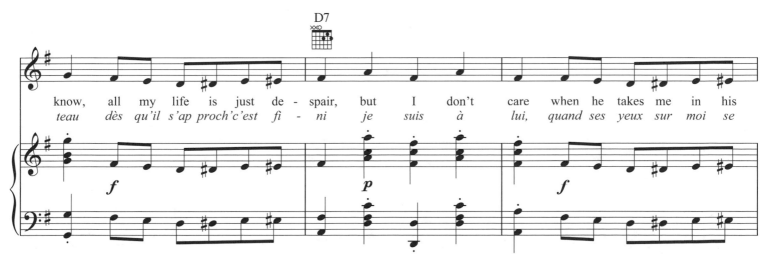

know, all my life is just de - spair, but I don't care when he takes me in his
teau dès qu'il s'ap proch'c'est fi - ni je suis à lui, quand ses yeux sur moi se

arms the world is bright, all right.

pos'nt ça m'rend tout cho - se,

What's the dif-f'rence if I say I'll go a - way, when I know I'll come back

Je l'ai tell'ment dans la peau qu'au moin - dre mot, j'm' f'rait fair'n' im - por - te

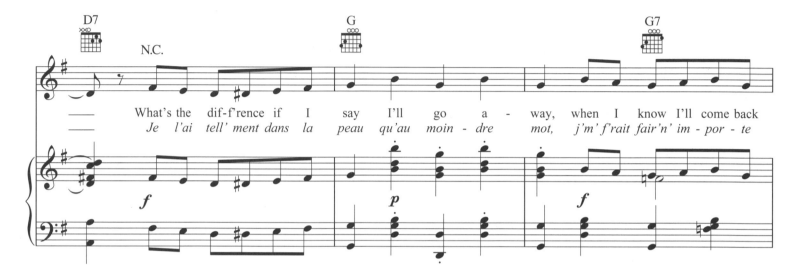

on my knees some - day? For what - ev - er my man is I am his for -

quoi. J'tue - rais ma foi, j'sens qu'il me ren - drait in fâme, mais je n'suis qu'un'

ev - er - more! Oh, my man I love him

fem - me. Et j'lai tell'ment dans la

NOW OR NEVER

Words and Music by
CURTIS LEWIS

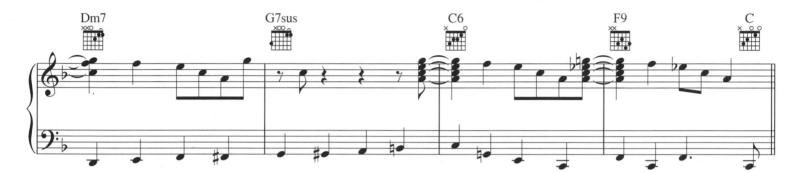

Hey there, dad-dy, make up your mind, 'cause I've been wait-ing such a long, long time.
call you once more on the tel-e-phone. I'll give you 'til twelve, and I'll be gone.
wait-ed last night for you to call; you give me no con-sid-er-a-tion at all. It's

Now, ba-by, or nev-er, 'cause I've been so good to you.
Now, ba-by or nev-er,
now, ba-by, or nev-er, 'cause you've wast-ed so much time.

Now, ___ ba - by, or nev - er, and it ain't no fault of mine. ___

___ It's got - ta be yes or no. It's ei - ther you

stay or go. You can't leave me on the shelf. You've got - ta com -

mit your - self. It's ei - ther you will, ba - by, or won't ___ fall in ___ love with

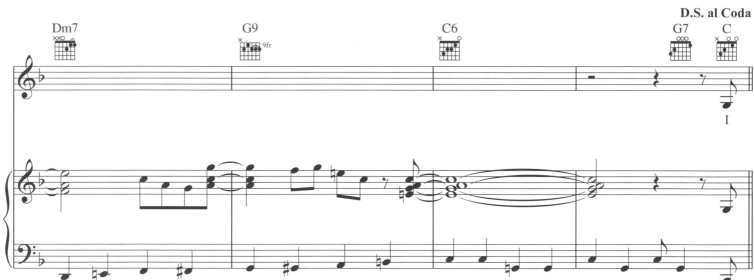

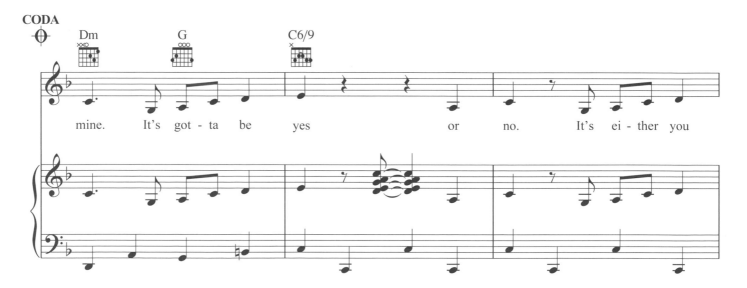

stay or go. You can't leave me on the

shelf. You've got -ta com - mit your - self. It's ei -ther you

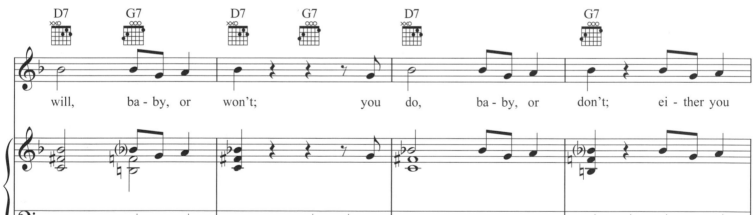

will, ba - by, or won't; you do, ba - by, or don't; ei - ther you

will, ba - by, or won't fall in love with me.___

SOMEBODY'S ON MY MIND

Words and Music by BILLIE HOLIDAY
and ARTHUR HERZOG JR.

Some-bod-y's on my mind, _____ like an old sweet song, _ the

last-ing kind. _ Some-bod-y's on my mind, _____ so I'm

walk-ing on clouds, _ all sil-ver lined. To dream my dream _

STORMY BLUES

Words and Music by
BILLIE HOLIDAY

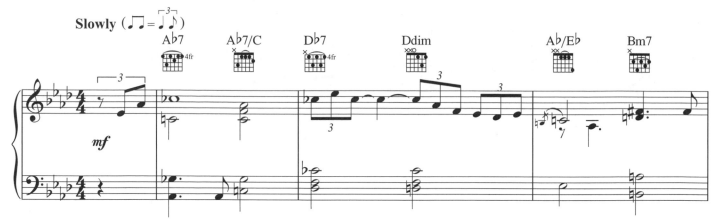

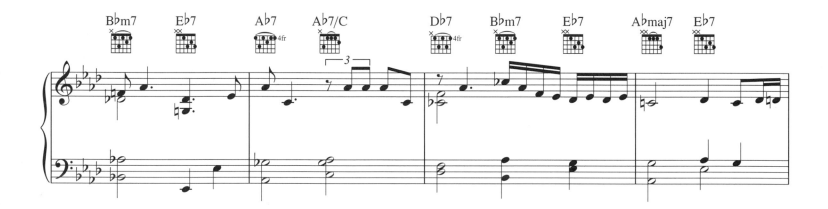

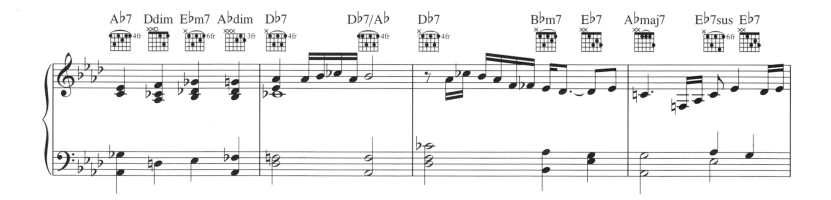

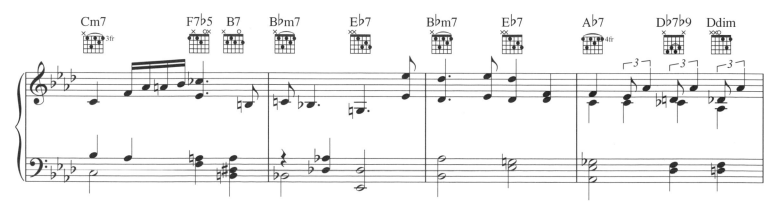

STRANGE FRUIT

Words and Music by
LEWIS ALLAN

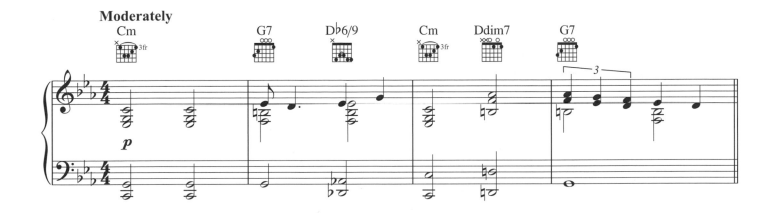

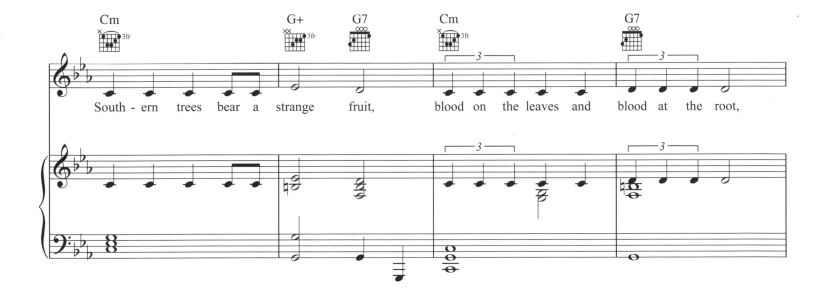

South-ern trees bear a strange fruit, blood on the leaves and blood at the root,

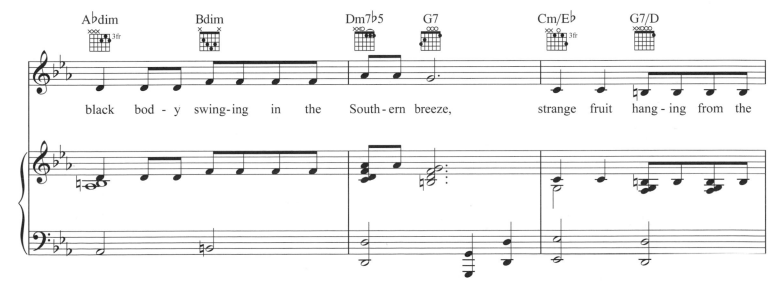

black bod-y swing-ing in the South-ern breeze, strange fruit hang-ing from the

STORMY WEATHER
(Keeps Rainin' All the Time)

Lyric by TED KOEHLER
Music by HAROLD ARLEN

Just can't get my poor self to - geth - er, _____ I'm wea - ry all __ the time, _____ the

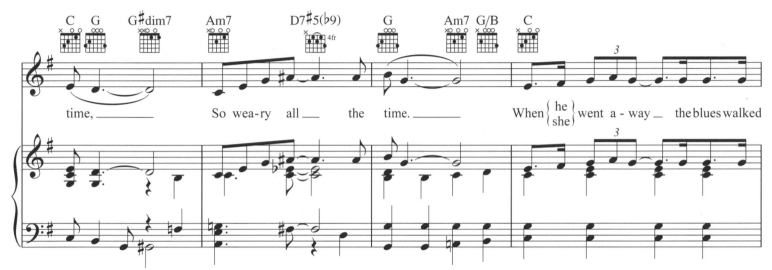

time, _____ So wea - ry all __ the time. _____ When {he she} went a - way __ the blues walked

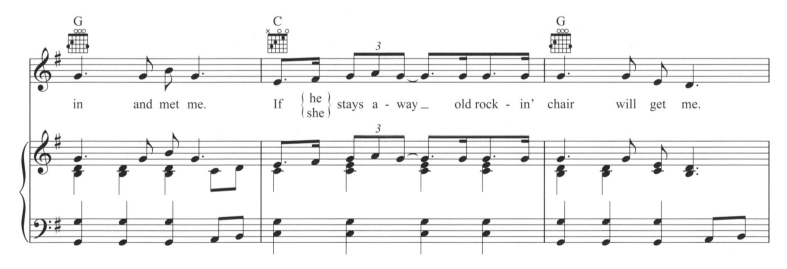

in and met me. If {he she} stays a - way __ old rock - in' chair will get me.

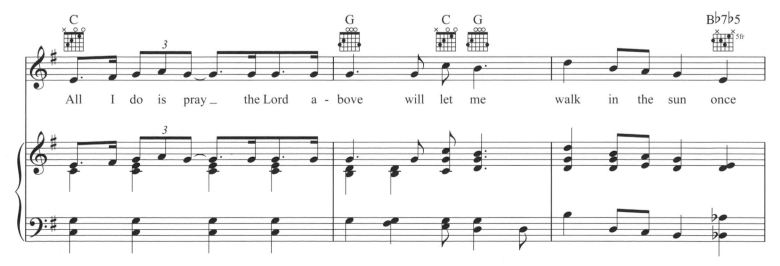

All I do is pray __ the Lord a - bove will let me walk in the sun once

TAIN'T NOBODY'S BIZ-NESS IF I DO

Words and Music by PORTER GRAINGER
and EVERETT ROBBINS

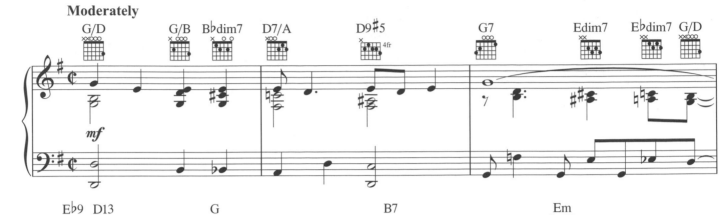

There ain't noth-in' I can do, nor noth-in' I can

Af-ter all, the way to do is do just as you

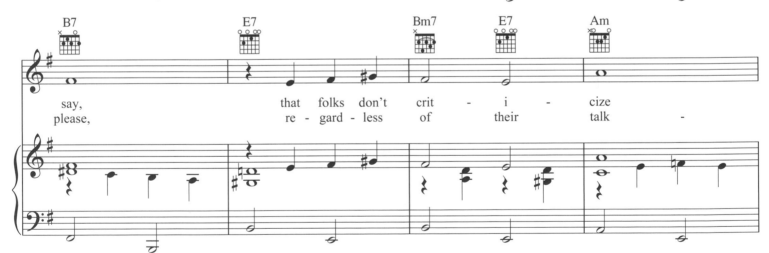

say,
please,

that folks don't crit-i-cize
re-gard-less of their talk

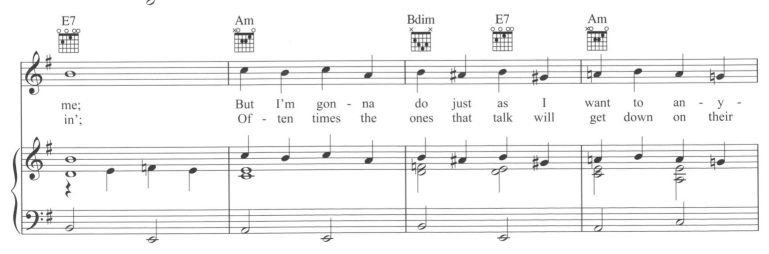

me;
in';

But I'm gon-na do just as I want to an-y-
Of-ten times the ones that talk will get down on their

way, and don't care if they all de - spise

knees, and beg your par - don for their squawk -

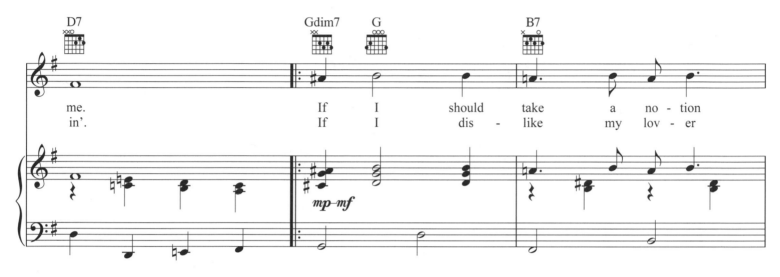

me. If I should take a no - tion

in'. If I dis - like my lov - er

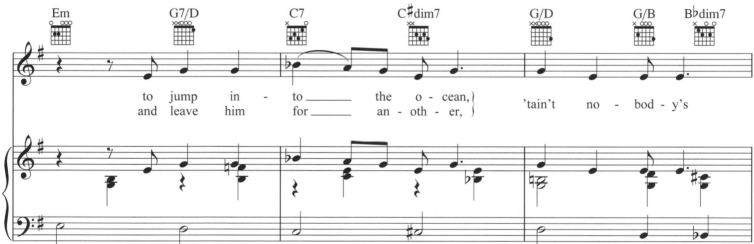

to jump in - to _____ the o - cean,}

and leave him for _____ an - oth - er,} 'tain't no - bod - y's

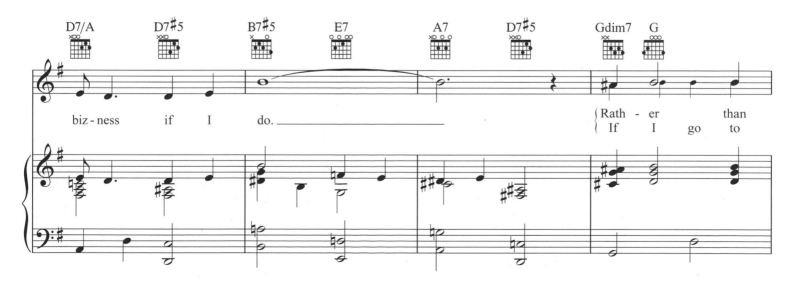

biz - ness if I do. _____ {Rath - er than

{If I go to

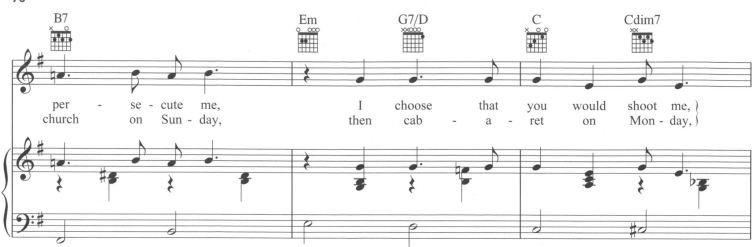

per - se - cute me, I choose that you would shoot me,
church on Sun - day, then cab - a - ret on Mon - day,

'tain't no - bod - y's biz - ness if ___ I ___ do. ___

If I should get the feel - in'
If my friend ain't got no mon - ey

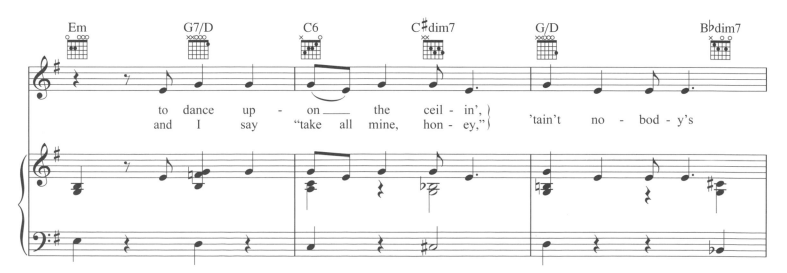

to dance up - on ___ the ceil - in',
and I say "take all mine, hon - ey," } 'tain't no - bod - y's

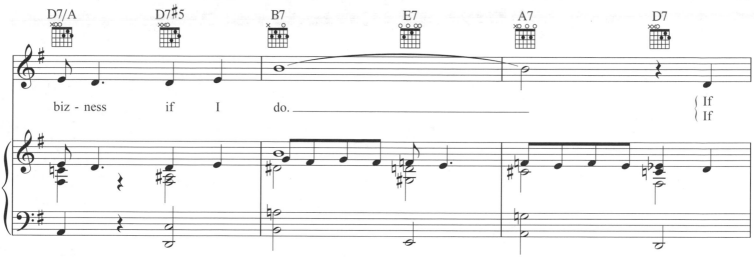

biz - ness if I do. _____ { If
{ If

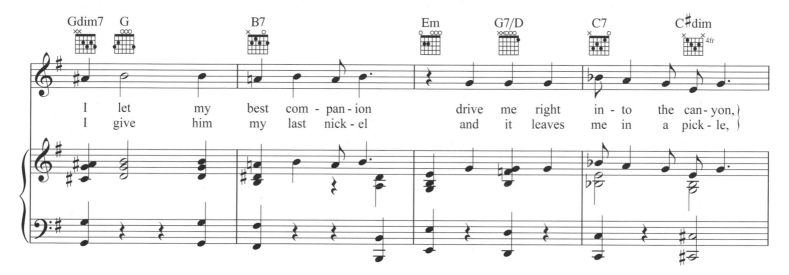

I let my best com - pan - ion drive me right in - to the can - yon,
I give him my last nick - el and it leaves me in a pick - le,

'tain't no - bod - y's biz - ness if ___ I do.

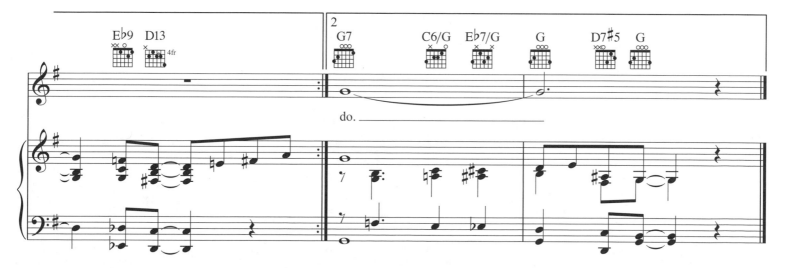

do. _____

THEM THERE EYES

Words and Music by MACEO PINKARD,
WILLIAM TRACEY and DORIS TAUBER

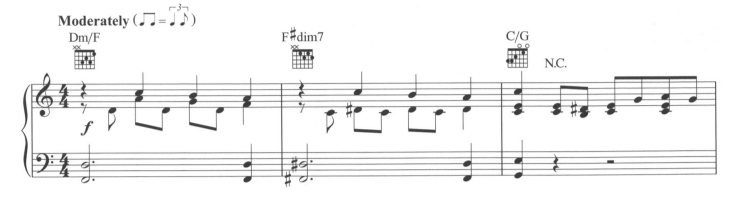

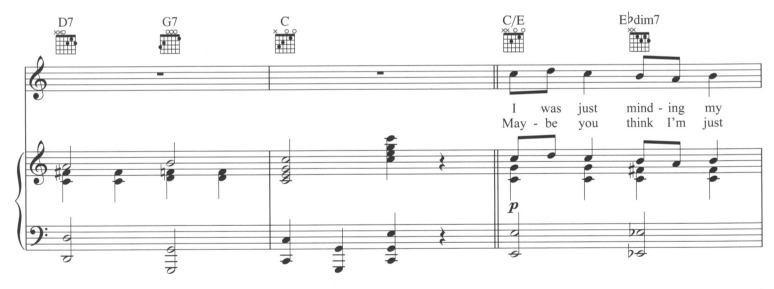

I was just mind-ing my
May-be you think I'm just

bus-'ness,
flirt-in',

life was a beau-ti-ful song.
may-be you think I'm all lies,

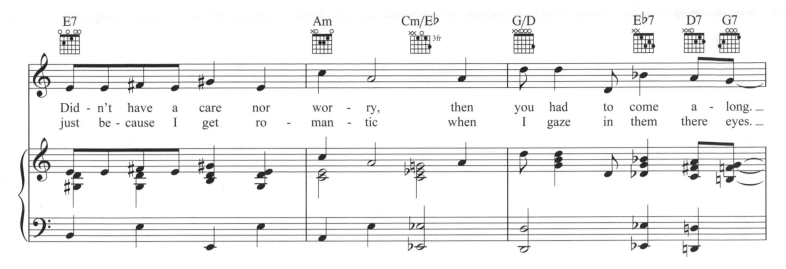

Did - n't have a care nor wor - ry, then you had to come a - long. __
just be - cause I get ro - man - tic when I gaze in them there eyes. __

I fell in love with you first time I looked in - to

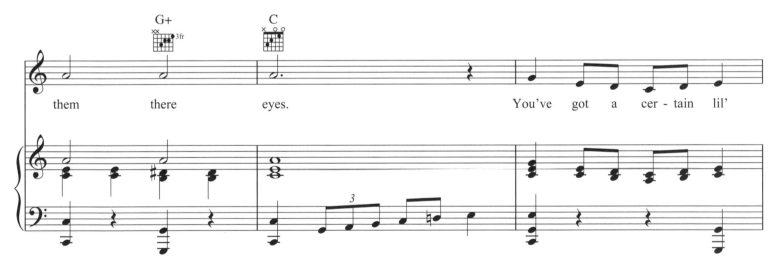

them there eyes. You've got a cer - tain lil'

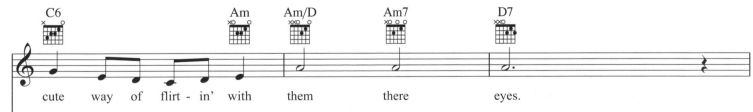

cute way of flirt - in' with them there eyes.

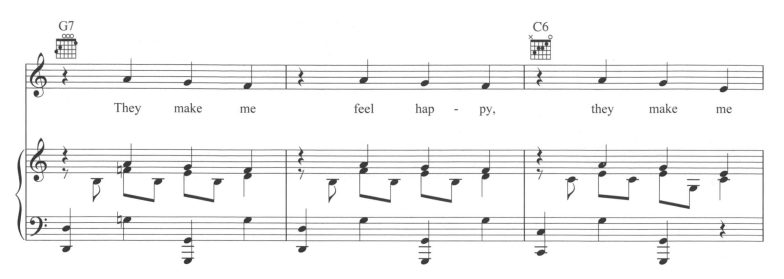

They make me feel hap - py, they make me

blue. No stall - in', I'm fall - in',

go - in' in a big way for sweet lit - tle you. My heart is jump - in', you

sure start - ed some - thin' with them there eyes.

You'd bet-ter watch them if you're wise. _____

They spar-kle, they bub-ble. They're gon-na get you in a

whole lot-ta trou-ble. You're o-ver-work-in' 'em, there's dan-ger lurk-in' in

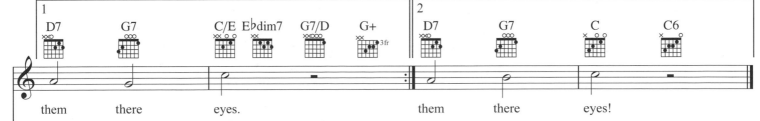

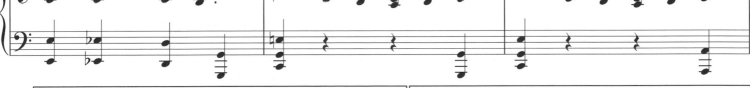

1
them there eyes.

2
them there eyes!

WHAT A LITTLE MOONLIGHT CAN DO

Words and Music by
HARRY WOODS

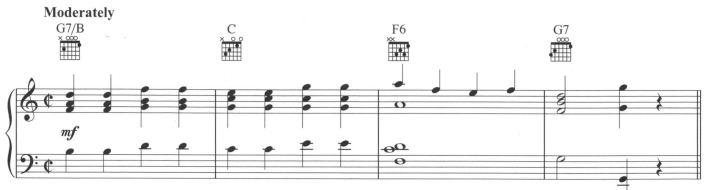

Ooh, ooh, ooh. _____ What a lit-tle moon-light can

do - o - o. _____

Ooh, ooh, ooh. _____ What a lit-tle moon-light can

do to you! _____ You're in love, __

__ your heart's a - flut - ter. And all day long ___

you on - ly stut - ter 'cause your poor tongue ___ just will not

ut - ter the words, "I love you."

Ooh, ooh, ooh. ___ What a lit-tle moon-light can

do - o - o. ___

Wait a while, ___ till a lit-tle moon-beam comes

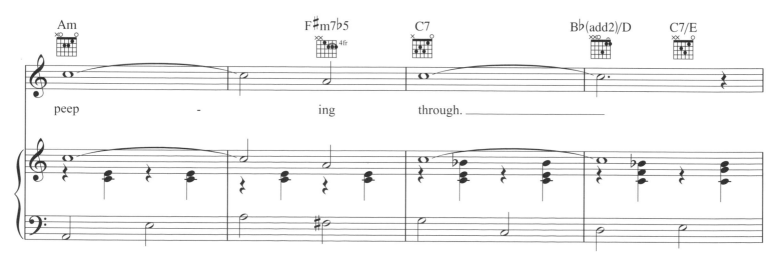

peep - ing through. ___

You'll get bold. ____ You can't re - sist her. And

all you'll say, ____ when you have kiss'd her, is ooh, ooh, ooh. __

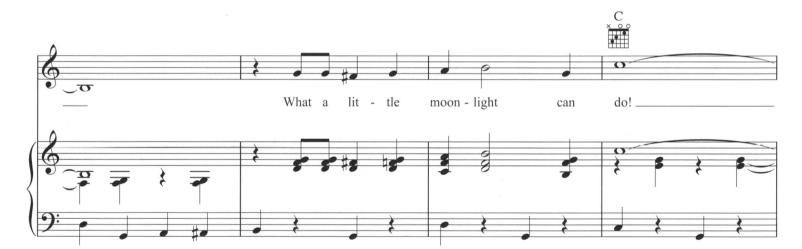

What a lit - tle moon - light can do! _____

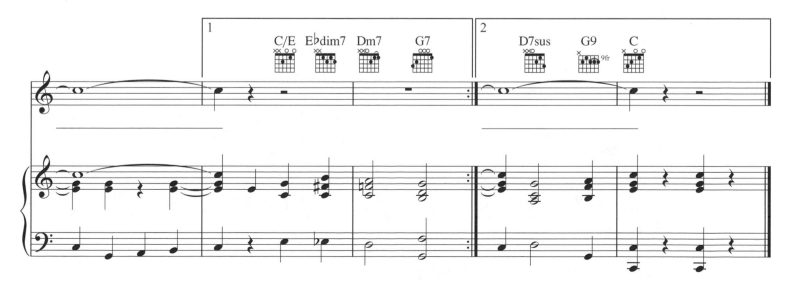

TELL ME MORE AND MORE AND THEN SOME

Words and Music by
BILLIE HOLIDAY

more and more __ and then some! _____ The way that you feel __ and then __

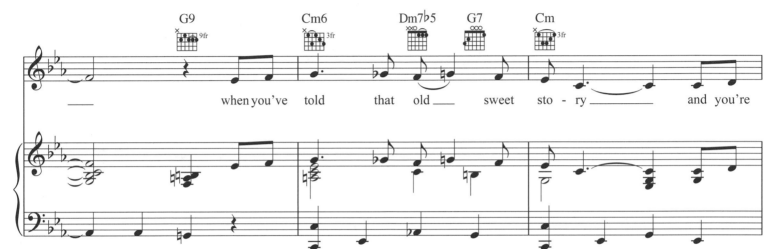

____ when you've told that old __ sweet sto-ry _____ and you're

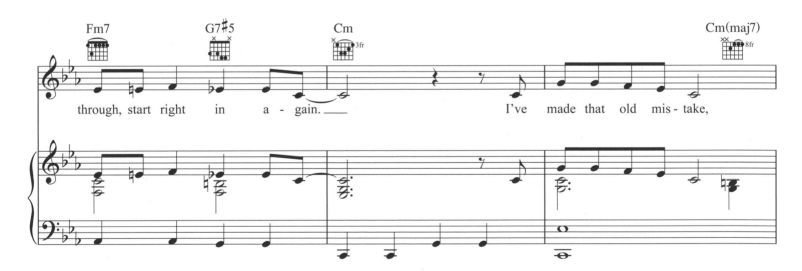

through, start right in a-gain. ____ I've made that old mis-take,

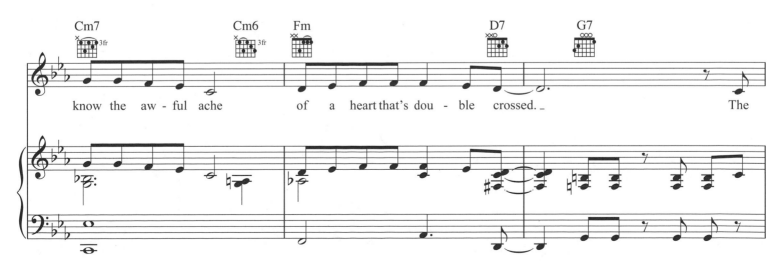

know the aw-ful ache of a heart that's dou-ble crossed. _ The

wait-in's been so long, hard to be be-liev-in' if I've missed my guess, hap-pi-

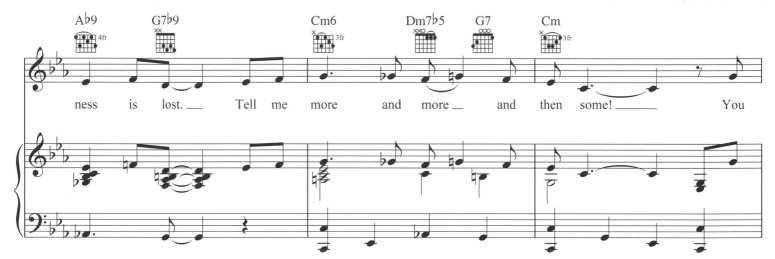

ness is lost.___ Tell me more and more ___ and then some! _____ You

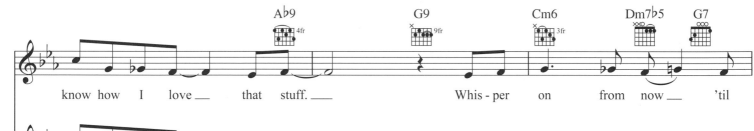

know how I love ___ that stuff. ____ Whis-per on from now ___ 'til

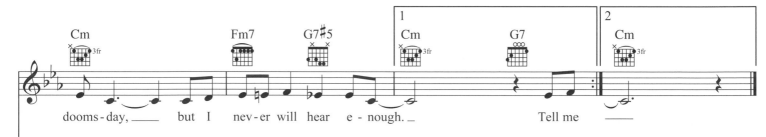

dooms-day, _____ but I nev-er will hear e-nough._ Tell me _____